Master Stress Management

Reduce Stress, Worry Less, and Improve Your Mood. Discover How to Stay Calm Under Pressure Through Emotional Resilience, Mental Toughness, and Mindfulness Techniques

Derick Howell

TABLE OF CONTENTS

INTRODUCTION... 1

CHAPTER ONE: 5

Stress 101: The Basics Of Stress

CHAPTER TWO: 17

Reduce And Manage Stress

CHAPTER THREE: 27

Identifying The Stressors In Your Life

CHAPTER FOUR: 37

Four Pillars Of Stress Management

CHAPTER FIVE: 45

How to Worry Less And Enjoy Life More

CHAPTER SIX: 55

How To Develop Emotional Resilience

CHAPTER SEVEN: 65

Powerful Ways To Build Mental Toughness

CHAPTER EIGHT: 75

Relaxation Techniques

CHAPTER NINE: 85

Mindfulness Techniques - Relieving Stress In The Moment

CHAPTER TEN: 95

Managing Stress At Work

FINAL WORDS 105

RESOURCES 109

YOUR FREE GIFT 113

INTRODUCTION

Say you're at your favorite café, reading this book, and as you glance up from taking a sip of your delicious coffee, you notice the people standing in line. Your attention wanders to the woman in a black dress, three people from the counter. Now, take a really good look at her. And I don't mean a simple glance -- I mean, really take your time to look at her. She is probably not missing fingers, covered in scars, or even looking sickly at all. She appears perfectly healthy, yet this doesn't mean that she is not suffering from a disease that you cannot see, like high cholesterol, high blood pressure, or some other disease. The diseases we get nowadays differ from what used to affect our parents or grandparents. The kind of diseases we get now also have different causes and consequences.

If a caveman inadvertently ate meat that was contaminated, the consequences were clear -- they would die a few days later. Now, when it comes to having a bad diet, the consequences are not as clearly defined. You could end up with a variety of conditions as a result of a poor diet, such as cardiovascular problems, obesity, diabetes, and so forth, that could affect the quality of your life. But this outcome depends on a lot of factors, including your genetic makeup, the type of junk food you consistently ate, how much junk food you ate, your personality, and your stress level.

Stress is everywhere and there is no way to avoid it. Whether you're stuck in traffic, late for work, have an approaching deadline, relationship problems, trauma, and so on, we have all been in stressful situations.

Ever noticed how your breathing quickens, your pulse goes up, and your muscles tense whenever something stressful happens? You may even get an energy boost and you are ready to take on whatever comes your way. While this might be great when you are in danger, it doesn't work when what's causing your stress is your three-year-old son or your demanding boss. What do you do then? How do you handle this stress?

Life has a lot of demands and every day more keeps coming up. These demands can either cause good or bad stress. I bet you didn't know that not all stress is bad. For instance, getting married or moving to a bigger house can be stressful. But most people don't see it as bad stress because these are good things. You are about to marry the love of your life, but planning the wedding took its toll on you. Moving requires you to pack, unpack, and rearrange everything so your new house truly feels like home. However, do you have the time to get this all done?

Unfortunately, many of us are aware that we suffer from stress, but we often feel that we have no control over it and we usually don't have the tools or skills to lessen its effects and manage our overall stress levels. Like many, perhaps you are in search of some effective methods and skills you can use to reduce your stress levels.

Whether you are aware that you are stressed, or you suspect that you could be, this is the book for you. It contains a wide range of well-detailed techniques and tips aimed at helping you reign in your stress and improve your functioning and focus, while also helping improve your quality of life. These techniques aren't only for stress reduction -- they are meant to teach you how to handle stress and build your resilience to it and its effects. This book has actionable steps that you can jump into right now and apply for a quick stress fix and others that seek to permanently take away the physical and mental pressures that stress causes, helping you regain control and changing how you react to it.

You could be wondering, how can I be so sure of these techniques? What proof is there that these exercises relieve stress? Well, I have been teaching people about stress and how to manage it for many years now. These tips and tricks are backed by research, extensive studies over many years, and personal experience.

People everywhere, myself included, have embraced these techniques and are experiencing their benefits. They worry less, have fewer mood swings and outbursts, and are calm under pressure because they have built mental toughness and emotional resilience. And the benefits don't stop there. Learning to reduce and manage your stress is good for you, both mentally and physically. It boosts your happiness and well-being and helps reverse some of the effects of stress, such as high cortisol and adrenaline levels.

I use mindfulness, breathing techniques, and meditation every day. I have to juggle a lot, so these skills help keep me sane and on track. Reading this book will not only change how you view stress, but also show you that managing stress is easy -- you just have to be mindful of it. These techniques will help you gain control of the emotions that seemed out of your control, such as anger, rage, or helplessness. They will change how you think, as well as your behaviors, habits, and actions, and teach you new ways of dealing with difficult situations.

As you read on, keep your mind open and allow me to help you as you equip yourself with the tools and skills necessary for stress management. Find a book and a pen and take note of the important concepts discussed in this book. Understand that you are no longer helpless in the face of stress -- you can take charge now! Nobody wants to live their life stressed and, while you cannot eliminate it from your life, you can master how to control it. The first step is by reading this book.

Happy reading!

CHAPTER ONE:

Stress 101: The Basics Of Stress

Think about it:

What's the first thing that comes to mind when someone says the word "stress"? Perhaps you think of your harsh boss and high-pressure job, your tattered finances, breaking marriage, or horrific event that happened to you years ago but still haunt you. Whatever your definition, the fact remains that most of us don't really know what stress is. We experience it from time to time, but when asked to define exactly what it is, we may be at a loss for words. In fact, most times, we only realize we are stressed when we are on the verge of breaking. So, what is stress exactly?

What is stress?

Defining what stress is can be hard since it is a highly subjective experience. However, the term stress, according to the American Institute of Stress, can be defined as the body's nonspecific reaction to any demands for change. Hans Selye conceived of this definition of stress in the year 1936. He was a Hungarian-Canadian endocrinologist who researched the hypothetical non-scientific response of organisms to stressors. He stated that stress was stressful, whether you received good or bad news or if the impulse was negative or positive. Hans Selye's research into stress began after he observed patients with chronic illnesses exhibiting similar symptoms, which he would later attribute to stress. He also observed this same phenomenon when lab rats were exposed to cold, drugs, or surgical procedures. They displayed a common set of responses, which he called General Adaptation Syndrome. This syndrome happened in three phases -- first, the initial "alarm phase", followed by a "resistance" or "adaptation phase", and eventually, exhaustion and death.

According to the Mayo Clinic, the alarm phase refers to the initial symptoms in the body when under stress. This fight or flight response prepares you to either flee or protect yourself in bad situations. In this stage, your heart rate increases, cortisol is released, which increases your energy, and your muscles tense, ready for what might happen. The second stage, or the resistance phase, comes after the fight or flight response when the body begins mending itself. Cortisol levels reduce and your pulse rate and blood pressure begin to go back to their normal levels. However, the alarm stage of stress states that even though your body has entered the recovery phase, it's still on high alert. If you dealt with your stressful situation and it is no longer an issue, your body will continue with its repairs, regulating your hormonal levels, blood pressure, and heart rate.

However, if your stress persists, your body will remain in this heightened state of alertness and it will eventually adapt to living with a higher stress level. Your body will then undergo changes you might not be aware of. Higuera notes that your body will continue secreting cortisol and other hormones and your heart rate and blood pressure will remain high. You may also exhibit irritability, frustration, and problems concentrating. If the resistance stage continues for too long without pause or cessation, it can lead to the exhaustion stage.

The exhaustion stage comes as a result of prolonged or chronic stress. It occurs when you have struggled with stress for too long that it has drained you physically, mentally, and emotionally and you no longer have the strength to combat your stress. According to Higuera, at this point, you might feel helpless, tired, or feel your circumstance is hopeless. In this stage, you might experience fatigue, burnout, depression, or anxiety, along with a decreased tolerance for existing or taking on new stress. Your immunity at this point is quite weakened, leaving you prone to opportunistic and stress-related illnesses.

This theory on stress and the GAS syndrome were derived from an experiment in which Higuera injected lab rats with various organ extracts. At first, he thought he had discovered a new hormone, but he quickly dispelled that theory after getting the same result, regardless of where he injected the substances. The adrenal cortex would swell and there would be a reduction in the functionality of the thymus, gastric, and duodenal ulcers. These results, combined with the prior observations he made about patients with different diseases displaying the same symptoms, led to his description of stress. He was also the first person to describe the body's stress coping system, the hypothalamic-pituitary-adrenal axis (HPA axis) system, which we will talk about later.

Felman, a writer for Medical News Today, says that whenever you feel threatened, your body releases chemicals that enable you to protect yourself from injury. These chemicals, cortisol, adrenaline, and noradrenaline can increase your heart rate, raise your blood pressure, and make you more alert. As I mentioned above, this reaction is known as your fight-or-flight response and is essential for survival. This heightened state fuels you to deal with the threat and improves your ability to handle the dangerous or challenging situation. Factors that can lead to stress are called stressors, the American Institute of Stress explains, and they can include noise, scary moments, your first day at work, fighting with your spouse, a speeding car, and so on. The more stressors we are under, the more stressed we tend to get.

This stress response, however, can sometimes be triggered too easily, for instance when we are subjected to too many stressors at once, as is the case with everyday life. Once the threat or change has passed, your body is supposed to revert to its normal, relaxed state. Unfortunately, the continuous, nonstop demands and complications of everyday, modern life mean that, for some people, their internal alarm systems never shut off.

Stress can mean various things to different people. What might be stressing you could be of little concern to another person. We get stressed

7

when the demands of life become too much and we struggle to cope with them. These demands can be anything from family and finances to your career, relationships, or any other situation that might pose a real or perceived challenge or threat to your well-being.

People also handle stress differently. Some are able to handle pressure, while others buckle under it. When we are faced with challenging situations, it is how we react to them that determines how much stress we will be under and the effects it will have on our health. If you feel that you might be lacking the resources needed to resolve your stressful situation, you might have a stronger reaction to stress, which can eventually trigger health problems, says Felman. If, on the other hand, you feel that you have the right resources to handle the situation, your stress levels are more likely to be lower with fewer health problems because of it.

Stress doesn't necessarily have to come from bad experiences or circumstances. As I mentioned above, even positive experiences, such as giving birth to a baby, taking a trip with your family, moving to a bigger, nicer house, or even being promoted can cause some stress. This is because there is a major change involved, extra effort is needed, or new responsibilities have come up and there is a need for adaptation. Having to step into unchartered territory and wondering how we will deal with this unknown can be stressful.

Like I mentioned before, not all stress is bad -- some of it is even beneficial and it can help save your life or help you perform better. It is the persistently negative response to a stressor that can lead to health problems and affect your happiness. However, if you are aware of your stressors and how you react to them, it can help lessen the adverse effects of stress and any negative feelings that might come up. This is where stress management comes in. Stress management gives you the tools you need to reset your internal alarm system. It enables your mind and body to adapt to long-term stressors and become more resilient to their effects. Without these tools, your body will always be on high alert and, over time, you could develop long-term stress that can lead to serious health problems.

Causes of stress

Stress is caused in part by two things, stressors and your perceptions, and it helps to know your stressors so that you can easily manage your stress. Factors or situations that lead to stress are referred to as stressors and many of us tend to think of stressors as being negative, such as a hectic work schedule or a problematic relationship. However, a stressor can be anything that demands a lot from you, including positive events.

Not all stressors come from external events, though. Sometimes, stress can be self-generated, for instance, when you worry about something that has a 50/50 chance of happening or not happening, fearing the unknown, having your beliefs challenged, or having irrational, self-defeating thoughts about life. These can include worrying that you will never be good enough, pretty enough, or smart enough.

Your perception of a stressor can also lead to stress. As mentioned before, a stressor to you might not be a stressor to someone else. Take, for instance, how public speaking terrifies most of us, while others crave the spotlight. One person might thrive under pressure and another might crack. These different reactions are because of our different perceptions of the situations. Other external exacerbators include major changes in your life or environment, workplace, social standing, losing a loved one, illness, family problems, lack of money or time, problems at work, driving in heavy traffic, uncertainty, or waiting on results, etc.

How your body reacts to stress

So now we know that stress can be positive or negative. Positive stress helps keep us alert and avoid danger, but when one is exposed to prolonged stress, it can become negative and you can end up overworked with stress-related tensions begin to build in your body. The body has an automatic stress coping system that kicks in, causing physiological changes that enable the body to deal with stressful situations. It is called the hypothalamic-pituitary-adrenal axis (HPA axis) system. This HPA axis system is a set of complex direct influences and feedback loops between the hypothalamus, pituitary glands, and the adrenal glands.

According to DeMorrow, in his 2018 International Journal of Molecular Sciences, these three organs form a major neuroendocrine system that controls the body's reaction to stress by regulating many of the bodily functions. These include digestion, the immune system, your moods and emotions, your sexual drive, energy storage, and use. It is the mechanism for interactions between your glands, hormones, and part of your midbrain that control the GAS syndrome.

Our bodies are made to experience stress and react to it. During a stress response, your body undergoes several changes, all because of the chemicals released. Since your body is about to face or handle something challenging, some of your bodily functions, such as digestion or your immune systems, are slowed since they are not very useful at the moment. All the focus is on increasing your oxygen intake and blood flow to your muscles, brain, and necessary body parts and ensuring your muscles are engaged. So you breathe faster, your blood pressure and heart rate are higher, your muscles become tense, and you enter a state of hyper-awareness.

When you are under stress for a long while, you enter a state called distress, which is when you get a negative reaction to stress. Distress can affect the body's internal systems, leading to problems such as headaches, ulcers, upset stomach, high blood pressure, loss of sexual drive, chest pains, and even sleeping problems. It can also cause premature graying of hair. There are also emotional problems caused by stress, which can include outbursts of anger, anxiety, depression, irritability, panic attacks, restlessness, and sadness.

You can also experience burnout, a general sense of unease, problems concentrating on what you are doing, fatigue, forgetfulness, and bad habits -- some people bite their nails to try and ease the anxiety within. Stress can also lead to behavioral changes, such as having food cravings, eating too much or too little, and losing your appetite altogether. Those under stress also tend to abuse drugs and alcohol, as they try to find an escape. They tend to withdraw socially, keeping to themselves and not engaging with family or friends and their relationships can fail because of this.

Research has also shown that stress can bring on or worsen certain conditions, such as heart disease, liver cirrhosis, lung disease, and even suicide. These conditions can be brought on by the various unhealthy ways we try to combat stress, such as abusing alcohol and other drugs. Instead of relieving the body of stress and returning it into a relaxed state, these substances offer temporary relief -- still, the body remains in an alarmed state, causing more health problems. This condition leaves people caught in a vicious cycle that can lead to death if it is not stopped.

Types of stress

Our bodies react to stress depending on whether it is new or short-term, also called acute stress, or whether it has been around for a while or long-term, referred to as chronic stress. These are the two main types of stress many of us face. Let's take a look at each one.

Acute stress

The Mayo Clinic website defines acute stress as temporary stress that goes away quickly and it is the most common way everyone experiences stress. It is caused by thinking about the pressure of things and events that have recently happened or what will happen soon. It is also called the fight-or-flight response and it is your body's immediate response to stressors, be it a perceived or real threat, challenge, or scare. It is an immediate, intense response and sometimes it can be thrilling, due to the release of adrenaline. It helps you manage dangerous or exciting situations. It is what you feel when you hit the brakes to avoid hitting something, or when you have a fast-approaching deadline. This type of stress reduces or completely ends once the stressor is resolved.

A single instance of acute stress is not harmful to your health -- it can actually be beneficial and doesn't cause the same amount of damage as long-term stress. However, it can cause tension, headaches, stomach problems, high blood pressure, and other mildly severe health issues.

Repeated instances of acute stress or severe acute stress can cause mental health problems, such as Acute Stress Disorder (ASD), and eventually lead to chronic stress. You can develop Acute Stress Disorder after being exposed to one or many traumatic events. An example of prolonged Acute Stress Disorder is Post-Traumatic Stress Disorder (PTSD). Symptoms of ASD can develop after witnessing traumatic or disturbing experiences, such as death or serious injury firsthand. These symptoms can start or get worse after the traumatic event and can last anywhere between three days to a month.

Examples of persons who might suffer from ASD include car accident victims, assault victims, or soldiers that have experienced war. Sometimes this can even develop into Post-Traumatic Stress Syndrome, which lasts longer than ASD. There is another form of acute stress known as Episodic Acute Stress that affects people whose stress triggers are frequent. For instance, if you have too many commitments and poor organizational skills, you can find yourself suffering from Episodic Acute Stress.

Dealing with acute stress

When your body's stress response is triggered by acute stress, you can reduce or reverse the effects by using quick relaxation techniques. These techniques are meant to help you relax quicker, feel less stressed, and recover faster from acute stress, so you can continue on with your daily activities.

To help manage your acute stress, you can try:

- Breathing exercises to help bring your heart rate down and slow your breathing.
- Cognitive reframing techniques, such as Cognitive Behavioral Therapy to help you change the way you view stressful situations.
- Progressive muscle relaxation methods, such as clenching and releasing different muscles to release tension.
- Mini-meditations to calm and center yourself and help you focus on the present moment.

Chronic stress

Chronic stress is stress that is experienced over long periods of time. It is regarded as the most harmful kind of stress because it eats away at us physically, mentally, and emotionally and we only realize that we have chronic stress once it is too late. It can cause burnout if it is not effectively managed because the stress response is triggered all the time and your body has no time to recover and repair itself before dealing with another wave of stress. This means that your stress response is triggered indefinitely, leaving you in an alarm state at all times, says Mayo Clinic staff.

This type of stress occurs daily, for instance, stressing over finances, an unhappy marriage, a dysfunctional family, or trouble at work. All these stressors can cause you distress daily because you don't see an end or an escape from these stressors. You eventually stop seeking solutions for these problems and resign yourself to fate.

Chronic stress can continue to go unnoticed, as we become used to the emotions generated and this heightened state, unlike acute stress, which is new and often has an immediate solution. This state of chronic stress can become part of your personality because you never deal with it, making you more prone to the effects of stress, regardless of the situations you might face. People with chronic stress are more likely to breakdown and even commit suicide or violent acts as ways of trying to cope with their stress.

Long-term stress can cause health issues, such as heart disease, gastrointestinal issues, panic attacks, anxiety, depression, and the other medical issues we mentioned before. This is why the management of chronic stress is crucial and it often takes a combination of short-term and long term techniques to relieve this kind of stress.

Dealing with chronic stress

With chronic stress, the body's stress response is prolonged, unlike with acute stress, and so the methods used to manage it must reduce the strain of stress on the body, giving it time to heal itself before it deals with more stress.

For chronic stress, you should:

- Exercise regularly to keep your body and mind healthy and also to release feel-good hormones to combat the stress hormones. You can try yoga, aerobics, Tai Chi, and other forms of exercise.
- Maintain a balanced and healthy diet that not only fuels your body but also helps boost your immunity and reduce your overall stress levels, so you can function better.
- Cultivate supportive relationships between family and friends, so you have a solid support system whenever you need it.
- Meditate deeply and often to help build your resilience to stress and also relieve acute stress.
- Other things you can do include listening to music because it calms the soul. Play with and stroke your pet -- this helps release feel-good hormones and it's a great mood booster.
- Practice mindfulness and positive self-talk to keep negative, self-defeating thoughts and emotions away.

Emotional stress is a type of chronic stress that can hit harder than other types of stress. Take, for instance, the stress caused when you fight with a loved one. It tends to cause a greater physical reaction and a more profound sense of distress than acute stress. It often leads to anxiety, anger, rumination, and other strong emotional responses that can take quite a toll on your body. Therefore, to manage it, you need to use a combination of techniques aimed at helping you process, diffuse, and gain emotional resilience toward these emotional stressors.

To deal with emotional stress, you can try journaling. A journal is a book where you can write down your thoughts and feelings surrounding occurrences in your life. As a stress management tool, it should be done consistently or even periodically, focusing on emotional processing and gratitude. You can write in detail about events happening in your life, your thoughts, feelings, and emotions and brainstorm solutions to what's bothering you. Whatever journaling method you choose depends on your personality, the time you have, and doing what feels right to you.

Managing chronic stress involves using these strategies, as well as some of the short-term stress-relieving techniques used for acute stress. Fortunately, it doesn't have to take stress ravaging and damaging your health, relationships, or quality of life for you to start practicing stress management techniques today.

CHAPTER TWO:

Reduce And Manage Stress

Now that you know what stress is, what causes it, the stages your body goes through while under stress, and the different types of stress, you can now move onto identifying different ways to reduce or manage the different types of stress you might be under. The first step is knowing what your triggers are. Once you have identified them, you can easily identify what you can control and start from there. For instance, if you have trouble sleeping because of stress, try reducing your caffeine intake and removing all electronics from your bedroom. This can help you wind down before bed. Other times, stress might be caused by work or the demands of an ill loved one. In these cases, what you can change is your reaction to the situation.

Stress-relieving methods

Stress can get you stuck in a bad cycle and the neural pathways in your brain can get stronger, making you sensitive to stressors and flooding your body with cortisol, adrenaline, and other stress hormones that it can't metabolize fast enough, notes Scott. What was intended to be an occasional stress response, quickly evolves into a daily occurrence, leaving your body stuck in any one of the three stages of the GAS syndrome. This prolonged period of stress can cause adverse effects to your physical and mental health and, without proper measures in place to reduce the effects, stress can lead to death.

Using quick stress relievers

Scott, in his article, An Overview of Stress Management, states that many different methods can be used to relieve different types of stress. Let's take a deeper look at some quick stress relievers. These methods or techniques are used to relieve stress fast and work in minutes to calm your stress response. When your stress response is not activated, you can deal with problems or situations more thoughtfully and proactively and you are less likely to lash out in frustration at others. This can be great for your relationships and interactions. Quickly dealing with stress can help reduce its effects and also prevent it from turning into long-term stress. These quick fixes may not build your resilience against future stress, but they can minimize the stress you are facing now and help calm your body after triggering the stress response.

1. Breathing exercises

An easy and fast way to bring your heart rate down and relax is by focusing on your breathing. Once the stress response kicks in, your breath can quicken due to the release of adrenaline and cortisol in your body. However, just focusing on your breathing can make a lot of difference and help bring down your stress levels. The intake of oxygen can help calm your body and mind in a very short time.

Take in deep breaths through your nose and fill your belly with air. As you inhale, slowly count to five, then hold your breath for about two seconds and slowly breathe out through your nose or mouth as you count to five again. As you breathe in, imagine that you are inhaling peaceful, energetic air, and it is spreading throughout your body, taking away the tension and stress. As you exhale, see yourself breathing out the stress and tension that has been washed away by the new peaceful air you took in.

2. Take a walk

Exercise is another great stress-relieving tool that can also work fast. When you take a walk, you get to enjoy the scenery and get out of your mind, on top of getting all the benefits of exercise itself. You don't have to take a long walk -- even short walks can help reduce stress. So, whenever you feel frustrated from work, take a short walk in the park during your break to rejuvenate your mind and body.

3. Progressive Muscle Relaxation (PMR)

PMR is an effective technique that helps reduce the body's tension, as well as psychological stress. This method involves tensing and relaxing the different muscles in your body, group by group. By doing this, you are releasing both physical and psychological tension. Research has shown that this method decreases your stress reactivity and your chances of experiencing chronic stress. It is also great for minimizing emotional stress and building resilience against stress.

How to do PMR

- Set aside some time and set the alarm so you can fully relax, not having to worry about losing track of time. Find somewhere private, so you can be more comfortable, whether you choose to sit, stand, or lie down. If you choose to lie down, stretch out and allow your body to have enough free space and to make circulation easier.
- Begin by taking deep breaths and tensing all the muscles in your face. Try and make a tight grimace, shut your eyes, and clench your teeth and hold this position for about five to ten seconds as you inhale deeply.
- Now exhale and relax your facial muscles. As you do this, you will feel all the tension flow out of your facial muscles. Take a few moments to enjoy the feeling before moving to the next step.
- Next, move to your neck and continue your way down to your toes, repeating whenever necessary until you feel all the tension is gone. You should experience a wave of relaxation sweep over your body once you are done. As you flex and relax your various muscles, you can change it up and do this for your whole body, causing it to relax rapidly. With practice, you can tell where there is tension or tightness in your muscles and be able to focus on them and relax more. This can then become your go-to

method for diffusing stressful situations, especially those that involve physical tension.

4. Try guided imagery

Guided imagery is a stress relief method wherein you picture yourself in your happy place, whether you are at the beach, at a spa getting pampered, or at your favorite restaurant. These images allow you to indulge in a vivid daydream, complete with all the emotions and thoughts. What makes guided imagery a great technique is that it can be done anywhere -- it is free, it takes very little to master the practice, and it provides immediate relief.

There are several ways you can practice guided imagery for stress relief. You can be guided by an instructor through audio or video recordings, or you can create your own visual recordings and use your inner voice as your guide. Guided imagery provides relaxation, insight into your subconscious, and leaves you stress-free with a positive mindset to boot. It can be a useful way to disrupt ruminating thought patterns and build your stress resilience.

5. Aromatherapy

Aromatherapy has been used over the years as a form of stress relief. Inhaling therapeutic aromas can help you energize, relax, and center. They have also been shown to alter brainwaves, allowing you to enter deeper states of relaxation while decreasing stress hormones in the body. Aromatherapy is favored in spas and other places of relaxation because it calms the body and helps release tension.

6. Get a hug

Physical touch from a loved one can help relieve stress fast. Getting a hug, for instance, is a simple way to cause the production of oxytocin, the cuddle hormone, which suppresses the production of norepinephrine, a stress hormone, reduces blood pressure, and causes you to feel good. Oxytocin is linked to higher levels of happiness and lowering stress.

also get tangible support, which involves someone else taking over your responsibilities so you can handle your problem. It can also be shown by someone taking a supportive stand with you and actively helping you deal with your issues. An example of tangible support would be someone bringing you lunch or dinner when you are ill.

6. Take time off

When you take time off, also disconnect from technology. While complete disconnection is perhaps not a feasible option, try taking some time off from your devices during the day and an hour before you go to bed. Looking at screens all day can throw your circadian rhythm off and make getting a good night's sleep hard. This disrupted sleep pattern can worsen stress symptoms and their effects.

7. Eliminating stressors

Stressors are everywhere, both internally and externally, and while completely eliminating them is impossible, you can remove the biggest stressors in your life. For instance, getting out of a bad marriage or relationship can lessen your overall stress and help you effectively deal with other areas in your life that might be stressing you, such as work. For areas where you can't eliminate the stressor, try to minimize it to a manageable level. For instance, if your job is very demanding and this is creating a stressful environment for you, try to delegate some of the workload or apply for a different, less demanding position. This way, you can reduce your stress because you are not as overwhelmed or overworked.

8. Try Cognitive Behavioral Therapy

According to *Psychcentral*, Cognitive Behavioral Therapy (CBT) is a type of psychotherapy treatment that aims to change how you react, your thought-patterns, emotions, behaviors, and habits towards stressors. It is a short-term form of therapy directed at current issues, such as stress, and is based on the opinion that how an individual thinks and feels influences how they behave. The goal of CBT is to solve problems, such as ASD, by changing how you think and feel in order to change how you react. It not only aims to help alleviate the symptoms of acute stress, it can also prevent you from developing PTSD.

During CBT sessions, you learn how to identify the painful or upsetting thoughts that trigger your stress response and you determine whether they are realistic or not. If they are deemed unrealistic, you are taught techniques to help you change your thought and emotion patterns so you can think and react more logically to a situation.

Other habits you can acquire include listening to music, learning to say no, journaling, getting quality sleep, making the most of your free time, and more.

Understand that it is impossible to remove stress from your life completely. However, by continuous stress management and paying attention to stressors in your life, you can counter some of the adverse effects of stress and increase your ability to cope with any challenges that might come up. There is no one-size-fits-all method of relieving stress. Whatever method works for you might not work for someone else, so take time to find the right combination of methods that are right for you.

CHAPTER THREE:

Identifying The Stressors In Your Life

Effectively managing your stress starts with first identifying what is stressing you and coming up with strategies to deal with them. The Mayo Clinic explains that knowing what creates your stress is the first step toward leading a healthier, less stressful life. Stressors or stress-inducing factors are the things that trigger your stress response. Identifying them sounds pretty straight forward, but sometimes getting to the bottom of your stress is harder than it sounds. With acute stress, it is easy to identify stressors, such as a job interview, a divorce, or any of the many reasons that cause short-term stress. However, with chronic stress, it can get a lot more complicated. To begin with, sometimes it is difficult to tell that you might have chronic stress until it is too late and you are already suffering its adverse effects. It is also easy to overlook our thoughts, emotions, behaviors, and habits as contributors to our overall stress levels.

Sure, sometimes you may be aware of the things you worry about, such as work deadlines, but maybe it could be your procrastination habit and not the demands of the job that are actually causing your stress. To truly identify your stressors, you have to thoroughly examine your thoughts, habits, attitudes, and behaviors.

- Do you find yourself rationalizing away stress as brief, even though you cannot remember the last time you relaxed? "I just have so much work to do right now."

- Do you describe stress as an integral part of your home or work life? "Things at work are always hectic." Or do you use it to define your personality? "I have nervous energy. I am wired like that, that's all."
- Do you blame your stress on circumstances or other people? "My boss is overworking me." Or do you view it as a normal occurrence? "It's nothing new -- working here is quite demanding, but I am used to it."
- Does any of this sound familiar? Until you accept the role you play in creating and maintaining your stress level, it will always be out of your control.

Olpin and Hesson, in their book "Stress Management for Life", explain that stressors can be divided into two broad groups, external and internal stressors. External stressors are events or things that happen to you, such as traumatic events, workplace stress, environmental factors, and so on. Internal exasperations, on the other hand, are the stressors that are self-induced. These include thoughts and feelings that come to mind and cause you to worry. These internal stressors can include your fears, anxiety, and lack of control. We can also divide stressors into smaller groups, which can help narrow down the stress-inducing factors in your life.

1. Emotional stressors

These stress inducers can also be referred to as internal stressors because they are self-induced. They can include fears and anxieties over unknown situations, such as worrying what kind of impression you will make on your first day at work or on a blind date or certain personality traits that you may have, such as perfectionism, pessimism, hopelessness, being suspicious or paranoid of people, and so forth. These internal stress factors can shape your thinking, your self-perception, and the perceptions you have about others. These stressors are very individualistic and how they affect people also differs from person to person.

2. Family stressors

These stressors include changes that occur in your family life, such as a change in your relationship status, a fight with a family member or child, expecting a baby, getting married, experiencing empty-nest syndrome (which occurs when your kids grow up and move out of the house), financial problems, etc.

3. Social stressors

These stressors come whenever you interact with others. They can include getting anxious over dating, attending a party or a social gathering, or publicly addressing people. Similar to emotional stressors, social stressors are also individualized. For instance, you may love speaking in public, but the mere thought of addressing people may cause your classmate to freeze or break out in hives.

4. Change stressors

These are the stressful feelings you get when it comes to dealing with important changes in your life. The changes can either be positive, such as getting married, moving to a bigger house, or having a baby, or negative, such as the death of a family member, a breakup, divorce, or getting fired.

5. Work stressors

These triggers are caused by the demands of your workplace, whether at home or an office, or your career. They can include tight deadlines, an overbearing, unpredictable boss or, if you work from home, endless family demands that interrupt your work.

6. Chemical stressors

These include any drugs, such as alcohol, caffeine, nicotine, or pills that you might be abusing in an effort to deal with your chronic stress. More often than not, these chemical stressors end up worsening the stress response.

7. Physical stressors

These include any activities that might overwork or tax your body, such as going long hours without sleep, not eating enough food, not eating healthy food, standing or being in an uncomfortable position for a while, too much exercise, pregnancy, disease, and many other things.

8. Decision and phobia stressors

Decision stressors involve any decision making instances that might cause stress, such as choosing a life partner, deciding to have a baby, career choice, etc. Phobia stressors include any situations you might get yourself in that you might be very afraid of, for instance, flying, being in small confined spaces, getting dirty, and so forth.

Other stressor categories include disease stressors, pain stressors, and environmental stressors. As you can see, there are several kinds of stressors that can induce a stress reaction from you. Using this list of stressor categories, list down all the stressors in your life and note where your main stressors lie. You might discover that some of your stressors fall into multiple categories.

Closely examine this list and decide what stressors are in your control and which are not. If having to clean your whole apartment on your day off is cutting into your leisure time, consider sparing some money for a cleaning service. If pressing your clothes is causing you to go to bed too late, consider sending them to the cleaners or buying wrinkle-free clothing. If these solutions seem a bit pricey, try and rearrange your monthly budget and allocate money for these services, so you can get more time to rest because your time is valuable, too.

As I have said, you cannot completely eliminate stressors, only reduce their strength or potency. For instance, if your workplace is too noisy, try getting some earplugs to reduce the volume and help improve your concentration. If you have to drive two hours through heavy traffic to get to work, consider carpooling, mass transportation options, or carrying a book or some music for the journey to work.

Start Journaling

I've already talked a bit about journaling and what it is. Journaling is a simple way of having a relationship with your mind. Journaling requires the use of the left side of the brain, which is the analytical and rational side. While your left side is preoccupied with writing down what happened, your right side, which is also your creative side, is free to wander. By allowing your creative side to flourish, you can find ingenious ways to deal with your issues and it can make a big difference in your daily well-being.

Keeping a stress journal can help you identify the stressors in your life and eventually help manage your stress. By writing down your perceptions and emotions, you can tell when something causes you to feel overwhelmed or stressed. Journaling can also help you identify hidden or potential stressors that you may be overlooking and could contribute to your chronic stress. It is theorized that writing boosts mental health by guiding us towards dealing with inhibited emotions, thus reducing inhibition stress. It helps us process difficult situations and events and also helps us come up with a coherent story about what happened, such as with an accident or other traumatic events. We are able to work through traumatic memories through repeated exposure to them and, once we are aware of them, we can start working on eliminating them.

Journaling has tremendous benefits. For some, it is a way of tracking food intake, in an effort to lose weight. Others use it as a historical account or record of their lives that they can share with others, while others use it as a way to deal with their depressive moods. In addition to journaling for these and more reasons, what makes journaling a great stress reducer is that you can organize your thoughts once you write them down and deal with feelings you had not fully realized you had.

Journaling clears your mind from thoughts that may be weighing you down or overwhelming you. By writing down your thoughts, you are essentially clearing your mind of all the clutter you have stored in your brain. You can sift through what is important and what you can disregard and stop paying mind to. Journaling also helps get rid of the negative, self-defeating thoughts that you have. Studies in the Psychological Science Journal have shown that writing down your thoughts and throwing away the paper you wrote them on is an effective way of clearing your head. This theory was tested on some students who suffered from negative body image issues. It was found that the students who wrote down their thoughts and threw away the paper were affected less by these negative thoughts. The physical act of throwing away the paper containing the thoughts was a symbolic act of disregarding these bad thoughts and thus clearing their minds of them. This can work for you too and it can help you feel better and deal with your problems once your mind is clearer.

Journaling helps facilitate problem-solving. Since it helps clear your mind, you can approach whatever issue you are facing with a clear, level mind. By writing down your problems or whatever is stressing you, you can detach from your feelings and effectively reflect on them. This thought reflection can spark ideas on how you can better deal with what is stressing you and eventually come up with possible solutions.

It can improve your physical health, too. A study conducted in 2006 showed that patients suffering from chronic illnesses who journaled about stressful situations experienced fewer physical symptoms than those who didn't. Researchers followed 112 patients who suffered from asthma and arthritis and asked them to journal for about 20 minutes every day for three days in a row about any emotionally stressful occurrence in their day or about their daily plans. Those who journaled showed a 50 percent improvement in their condition after about four months.

Journaling also helps improve your working memory. As you write down the details of your day, traumatic experience, or stressful situation, you are essentially reliving it. By writing down what happened, you are able to capture a lot of detail of what happened. This is especially useful when dealing with traumatic stressors. By retracing your trauma or the events that lead to it, you can pinpoint what may be triggering your current stress response. You become more self-aware and you can easily detect unhealthy thought-patterns, emotions, and behaviors. Now you can regain control over your life and you can shift from a negative mindset to a more positive one by effectively dealing with the stress-inducing agents in your life.

When it comes to journaling, there are no definitive rules about how you should go about it. What is important is to find your rhythm by doing what works for you, whether this means journaling daily, weekly, or monthly. However, for this method to work, you need to be consistent. When you start off, you may need to journal more often to help you identify your stressor and also to help you deal with your emotions and effectively reduce your stress. As you go on, you can reduce the frequency to once a week since you already know what is causing you to stress and you have put in measures to mitigate this recurrent stress. You can carry around your journal to help you deal with instances of acute stress in combination with other quick stress fixes.

Whenever you feel the pressure coming on and you are getting stressed, write it down in your journal. Note down:

- What happened.
- What you think caused your stress (if you don't know, try and make a guess).
- How you felt about the event. What you experienced, both physically and emotionally.
- How you responded to what happened.
- What you did after to help you calm down and feel better.

This log will help you see patterns and recurrent themes in what causes your stress.

However, while writing down everything may feel good, to really reap the benefits of journaling and help reduce stress and keep other mental health problems at bay, you have to journal constructively. Here are some tips to assist you.

a. Whenever you can, find a private, personalized space to journal that is free of distractions.
b. Like I mentioned before, start journaling at least three to five times a week and try and be consistent and consecutive.

c. Give yourself enough time to think over and reflect on what you wrote. Take this time to balance yourself by reigning in your emotions.

d. If you are journaling about a traumatic event, don't feel pressured to recount the event in detail. You can just write about how it made you feel and how you feel now.

e. Structure your writing however you want. You can use past or present tense, notes, bullet points, or just write endlessly.

f. Keep your journal private. It is meant for your eyes only, not your spouse, parents, or friends. Not even your therapist should go through your journal, but you can talk about your experiences in your therapy sessions.

If you are baffled and don't know where to start, here are some topics to help you begin.

- An unforgettable time in your life, whether good or bad.
- If you could have three wishes, what would you wish for?
- What is your purpose in life?
- Write about a childhood memory and how it made you feel.
- Think about where you'd like to be in two or five years.
- What are your dreams, hopes, or fears?
- Where did you think you would be five years ago? What did you value at the time? Is it still important to you?
- What are you thankful for? You could start with just one thing, big or small, and go from there.
- What aspect(s) of your life require changing or elimination?
- How are you feeling mentally, physically, and emotionally?
- What challenges are you dealing with now?

- Think of the best and worst-case scenario that could happen to you right now. How would you react?

You can also use these simple guidelines to help jumpstart your thoughts. Think of the acronym W.R.I.T.E. whenever you want to start journaling.

i.   W: What would you like to write about? Think about your thoughts, emotions, where you are in life at the moment, current events, or things you are striving toward or trying to avoid. You can use some of the topic ideas I mentioned before.

ii.   R: Review what you wrote. Take time and go over what you wrote while calming yourself with a few deep breaths or some meditation. Try and keep your thoughts in the present by using statements such as "I feel...", "Today..." or "Here..."

iii.   I: Investigate and explore your thoughts and feelings through your writing. Don't stop writing, even when you run out of things to write. If your mind seems to be wandering, take a few moments to refocus, go over what you wrote, and continue.

iv.   T: Time yourself to ensure you journal for about ten minutes, or for however long your current goal is.

v.   E: Exit with a strategy and introspection. Go over what you wrote and think over it and summarize it in a few words. For example, "As I read this, I notice that..." You can note any actions you might want to take below.

Once you identify and organize your stressors, it gets a lot easier to deal with them.

CHAPTER FOUR:

Four Pillars of Stress Management

Too much stress in your life is not good. When it becomes too much, you need to find a way to eliminate or cope with it. Coping mechanisms give you a way to hit reset and restore yourself to normal. When dealing with predictable stressors, you can react in two ways: either change the situation you are in or how you react to the situation. When working out how to react to these stressors, it helps to think of the four pillars of stress management. In his book, "The Mindful Way Through Stress", Shamash Alidina writes that the four pillars of stress are: Avoid, Alter, Accept, and Adapt. These are also referred to as the 4 A's of stress management and they are designed to help you decide which option to select in any given scenario. Let's take a more in-depth look at what each of them entails.

Avoid

Even though it is not possible to avoid every stressful situation in your life, you'd be surprised how much stress you can avoid simply by eliminating or avoiding unnecessary stressors in your life. You can significantly impact your mental health by applying this simple skill. There are several ways you can avoid stressors and improve the quality of your life in the process.

■ Learn to say "no" – The first thing you must do is to know your limits and learn to stick to them. You must know how much you can take on before you start feeling overwhelmed, or the pressure becomes too much. This pertains to your professional and personal life. If you take on more than you can handle, you will end up stretched thin, tired, and overwhelmed, making this a great recipe for stress. You must distinguish between the 'shoulds' and the 'musts' in your life, so you can know when to say no and avoid taking on too much.

For instance, if your boss often asks you to work overtime and you never get to spend any time with your family, this can cause strain on you and your family. You can avoid this potentially stressful situation by saying no to working overtime too often. If you cannot take on any extra work at a particular time because you are already occupied, saying no can help you have enough time to clear your plate. You can also drop, delegate, or postpone any extra work you might have and focus on a bit at a time.

■ Avoid people who induce stress in your life -- by now, you already know the various ways in which you can identify potential stressors in your life. These stressors can sometimes be people and dealing with human stressors is the biggest challenge we face when eliminating stress. If you identify certain persons in your life as stressors, you should work to limit your time around or with them. Ending the relationship is another viable option you should also consider. For instance, if you are in a toxic relationship or marriage, consider leaving your significant other if you are suffering from stress and other stress-related illnesses.

■ Take more control of your environment -- your surroundings are a big piece of your life and the things in it can be the culprits behind your long-term stress. These environmental factors include watching the news, heavy traffic, running late for work, leaving the office late, and so on. By staying away from these stressors, you are able to avoid triggering your stress response. If the news is too depressing, you can choose not to watch it, if traffic is always making you late, you can use other forms of transportation or carpooling and so forth.

- Go through your to-do-list and reduce your workload. Closely examine the list of things, tasks, and responsibilities you have. If you are trying to handle too much, you will be overwhelmed, so look at what you should prioritize and work on that first. You can get to the other tasks in due time. Much of the stress we feel doesn't come from having too much to do but instead from not finishing what we started out doing. Be careful not to procrastinate, as this will only worsen your situation and leave you with a huge list of things that still have to be done.

Alter

If you cannot avoid a stressor or a stressful situation, you can try to alter it. This means that you will have to change either the way you communicate or operate in your daily life. During stressful times, you should make changes that positively impact your stress levels. Here are a few ways Alidina states you can alter the stressful situation you are in.

- Convey your feelings rather than bottling them up -- Dealing with how things make you feel when they happen can go a long way in reducing your overall stress levels. If someone or something is troubling you, be more assertive and convey your issues in a calm, open, and respectful manner. Communicate using "I" statements when requesting others to change their behavior. For instance, "I feel infuriated by what you did." "Can you help me handle this situation?" If you have a nearing deadline or a heavy workload and your coworker is getting chatty, let them know that you only have a bit of time to talk, and then you have to get back to work. Try delegating tasks and other responsibilities whenever possible. If you fail to express your feeling and bottle them up, you will build resentment, and this will only worsen your stress.

- Respectfully ask others to change their behavior – You should also be willing to do the same. By doing this, you can avoid turning small problems into big ones if they aren't resolved. For instance, if you are tired of being the butt of your coworkers jokes at the office, ask them to leave you out of their comedy routine, and you may be inclined to enjoy their jokes more.

■ Compromise – If you ask someone to change, you should also be willing to do the same. If you can meet each other halfway, then there is a good chance that you will work everything out and find a happy middle ground. For instance, if you are overwhelmed by work and chores at home, talk to your spouse about them helping out to help ease your workload. This can include getting the kids from school or getting dinner ready if you are running late. If something is not getting done how you would like it, rather than making a fuss and doing it yourself, try and talk to whoever is responsible and see how you can work things out. Let's say you are remodeling your bedroom, and you want to do it in a particular style; however, your spouse wants it in another style. Instead of arguing about whose style is better, find ways to incorporate aspects of both styles in the room. This will show that you respect their choices while still getting what you want and will also make everyone happy.

■ Balance your schedule – If you focus too much on work and don't slot in time for family or to rest and relax, you will soon burn out. It is, therefore, essential that you find a balance between your work and family life, solo pursuits and social activities, daily responsibilities, and your free time, and so forth. Focusing on one area can cause you to neglect the rest, and this can cause tension, frustration, and, eventually, stress. For instance, if you work a lot and never have time for your family or spouse, it can lead to them feeling frustrated, resentful, and abandoned. This can cause fights and make your home a hostile environment rather than a place you can relax. Working too much can also overwhelm you since you never have time to rest and cause you to burnout. Always ensure that you slot in enough time for all aspects of your life, family, work, social life, hobbies, etc.

- Seeing only the bad – this is when you seem only to notice what went wrong, rather than what went right. For example, "I got the last question wrong. I'm such an idiot."
- Finding ways to put down your positive moments like they don't count – you often downplay your wins, saying it was luck or you failed less than others.
- Believing that your feelings reflect reality – "I made a mistake during my presentation. Everyone must think I am a fool."
- Making negative leaps without any evidence – "I know something is going to go wrong." You act like you know what will happen, or like you can read minds, "I know they will hate me."
- Defining yourself based on your mistakes or perceived lack of skills.
- Taking responsibility for things you have no control over. "It is my fault that my husband had an accident. I should have done something to warn him."

To challenge them, you can follow the steps listed below.

- Give yourself time to worry.
- Determine whether your worry is fact or fiction.
- Can you view it more positively?
- Is the thought helpful? How will worrying help me find a solution?
- Ask whether you have control over it.
- If someone close to you had this worry, what would you say to them?

Talk to someone about what's worrying you

Talking about your feelings or what's on your mind with a trusted friend or family member can relieve some of the worry and anxiety you might be feeling. As the saying goes, a problem shared is half solved. So find someone to confide in and tell them about your worries. You can talk to a counselor or a therapist if you don't want to talk to someone close to you.

There are a few reasons that might make you a bit hesitant about opening up, such as not wanting to worry those close to you, or you may wish to keep your worries confidential, as sharing them might make you seem weak. You could also be lacking time to meet up with anyone because you are too busy. Whatever the reason may be, opening up can be beneficial to both your physical and mental health.

An experiment was conducted at the University of Southern California to measure the benefits of talking about your worries with someone else. They split participants into two groups and had one share their worries about making a speech while being recorded and the other participants weren't given this opportunity. Those who talked about their worries were found to have significantly lower levels of cortisol in their bodies than those who didn't. The researchers also found that those who shared their worries with other participants had the lowest cortisol levels.

According to Andrews, what this indicates is that sharing your worries with someone will greatly lower stress hormone levels in your body and sharing them with someone who was or is in a similar situation will give the best results. So if you have relationship worries, you can ease them by talking to someone who has been through them or something similar.

Practice accepting uncertainty

Self-help author Susan Jeffers notes in her book "Embracing Uncertainty" that life is random and you can never know how things will play out, but worrying about them is not the answer. Many of us think of uncertainty as something dangerous and that doing nothing about it is irresponsible. So we worry, trying to find ways how we can eliminate this uncertainty. However, worrying about the unknown is only helpful if it helps you think of ways you can cope. This is rarely the case because, as you think about the unknown, you only come up with more bad thoughts. You'll end up stuck in a loop because you keep coming up with more problems as you try to find solutions to others. These thoughts end up making you feel worse about what you are worrying about.

Professor Michael Rutter theorized that resilience is an interactive process involving exposure to toxic stressors that has a positive outcome for the person facing it. He also found that being briefly submitted to major stressors, such as getting fired, a disaster, or being separated from a loved one can trigger and influence one's resilience. His findings supported the possibility of the part genetics play in the amount of resilience one is born with.

Norman Garmezy found that our differences as individuals play a major role in determining one's resilience level. Family, community and social surroundings can affect your temperamental abilities and mold how you view and react to stress. Lastly, he theorized that interventions to develop or strengthen resilience must encompass all individual and environmental factors since addressing one doesn't help in building overall resilience.

Dr. Emmy Werner was the first person to discover that resilience is a variable that changes over time and differs depending on age and sex. She determined that depending on our age or sex, we are likely to react with different levels of resilience to varying stressors.

Dr. Michael Ungar came up with the concept of the "7 Tensions" that test our emotional resilience. He stated that they are present in all cultures, but how we react to them is affected by our cultural beliefs. These 7 Tensions are Material Resources, your Identity, Cultural Conformity, your Relationships, Social Justice, Cohesion, and lastly, Autonomy and Control.

These theories have affected how we view emotional resilience and also play a part in how we work to develop it.

Buddha once said that the secret of being mentally and physically healthy is not to mourn the past, worry over what is to come or anticipate problems, but to live earnestly and wisely in the present moment. To do so, we need to:

- Foster self-acceptance
- Improve our stress management skills
- Build our self-esteem

- Be mindful, focused, and aware of the present
- Be wise when expressing emotions
- React to stress in a way that doesn't affect us or those around us.

Here are some exercises you can use to develop your emotional resilience:

a) The power of positive thinking

Take some time and write down a few thoughts that are worrying you. Next to this column, Chowdhury suggests to write down a positive thought to replace it. For instance, "I am having trouble with my finances" can be replaced with "I should get financial guidance from friends, family, or an expert." Or, "I won't be able to do this" can be replaced with "Let me try, what's the worst that can happen." This is a simple way of showing how easily you can change your perspective on things.

b) Fostering gratitude

Gratitude is a pretty powerful emotion that comes when we learn to appreciate what we have, instead of complaining and fussing over what we don't have or lost. A lack of gratitude keeps us from advancing and decreases our ability to bounce back. Try keeping a gratitude journal, where you list everything you are grateful for, even during stressful times. Filling in the journal will help remind you that there are good things in life that are worth living for. For instance, you can start by writing down goals you have accomplished this week, what you might have that others lack, reasons why you are grateful to your family, ten good things that happened to you, and so on.

c) Gaining self-awareness and assessing yourself

Self-awareness entails knowing how our minds work by getting a deeper understanding of what led to a particular situation, how we choose to react to it, and the consequences of our reactions and the emotions they elicit. Make a list with four columns with the first showing the stressor, its cause, your reaction, and the consequences. Identifying and intrinsic, self-related mental, and emotional processes. Repetitive speech practices were shown to cause a significant reduction in obsessive thought processes and created a long-lasting calming psychological effect in individuals who practiced mantra related meditation.

Benefits of building mental strength

1. You gain emotional stability, which allows you to make better decisions when under pressure. It helps you maintain your ability to remain objective and perform as you normally would, despite how you feel.
2. It helps you gain perspective and be able to push through tough situations. It helps you keep your eyes on the prize through adversity.
3. With mental strength, you readily embrace change because you understand that it is inevitable. As you build your mental strength, you also develop adaptability and flexibility in how you think.
4. Mental toughness allows you to detach from a situation and understand that it is not about you. Rather than wasting time thinking why all this is happening to you, you can use that time to focus on what you can control, such as how you react.
5. It helps you develop resilience, which strengthens you and helps you better handle stress, anxiety, and fear. It also prepares you for challenges and adversity by helping you accept emotions and retain control over them. You are able to retain your focus and develop the right attitudes toward obstacles and uncertainty.
6. You can focus on doing what is best for you because you are not worried about pleasing others or what they think of you. This sense of self-confidence and self-reassurance is because you are mentally strong.
7. You exercise more patience in your actions and you don't act on impulse. Whenever our emotions are high, we tend to make rash decisions. As you build your mental capacity, you begin to understand that anything worthwhile takes time and you need to

work at it. This refers to accepting that you are a work in progress and that is okay.

Daskal notes in her article "18 Powerful Ways to Build Your Mental Toughness" that by applying these tips, you can build your mental strength and get a step closer to gaining control over your stress.

CHAPTER EIGHT:

Relaxation Techniques

Relaxation, for most people, means kicking back, lying on the couch and zoning out as you watch some TV after a long day. This type of relaxation, however, does very little to reduce the effects of the stress you have been under all day. Instead of activating your body's relaxation response, it merely distracts you from dealing with the stress. Stress can cause a lot of damage to your body if left unchecked, which is why you must find ways to cope with your stressors and manage your stress. There are several ways to cope with stress and one of them is through relaxation techniques. These techniques aim to trigger your body's relaxation response.

Remember that no single relaxation technique works for everyone because we are all different. Therefore, you must find the right method for you. It should be something that resonates with you, fits your style, and lets your mind trigger the relaxation response. Finding it may require some trial and error, but you will find the best method or combination of methods for you. Once you do, you can employ it or them to help manage your stress and anxiety, boost your mood and energy levels, and improve your health, in general. Practicing these relaxation methods, even for a few minutes a day, can calm you and help mitigate your stress.

The relaxation response

The relaxation response is a term that was coined by Dr. Herbert Benson, a cardiologist, author, professor, and founder of the Harvard Mind/Body Medical Institute. He defined this response as a person's ability to elicit their body to trigger brain signals and release chemicals that slow down their organs and muscles while increasing blood flow to the brain. It is the opposite of the fight-or-flight response, our survival mechanism, which is triggered when we are feeling overwhelmed, anxious, fearful, or stressed.

In chapter one, we talked about what happens when our bodies go into fight-or-flight mode. Our heart rate goes up, our blood pressure rises, and cortisol, adrenaline, and other stress chemicals are released. These chemicals increase our energy and cause our muscles to tense in readiness for what might happen. However, if this heightened state persists, it can have damaging effects on the body. This is why we must mitigate it by triggering the relaxation response.

In the article "Using the Relaxation Response to Reduce Stress", MacDonald notes that the relaxation response occurs when our bodies are no longer in danger, whether real or perceived, and body functions return to normal -- that is, our pulse and blood pressure go down, our breathing slows down, and our muscles relax. During the relaxation response, your body moves from being physiologically aroused or alert to a calmer state. This calm is achieved by reversing what the stress response triggered.

- Your heart rate and blood pressure are lowered.
- Your digestive and immune functions are brought back to normal.
- There is increased blood flow back to your extremities.
- Cortisol, adrenaline, and other stress hormones stop being released.

Inducing the relaxation response

During ancient times, our stress response helped us survive. It was triggered somewhat rarely, whenever we were in danger from threats, such as predators. However, nowadays, it is triggered a lot more often, even multiple times a day and we never have a chance to calm down and let our bodies recover from it. It is during such times that inducing the relaxation response can help calm the body and mind. According to Scott, the author of "Relaxation Response for Reversing Stress", this can be especially helpful when dealing with chronic stress. The body is in a continuous state of physiological arousal and the body doesn't have time to relax before the next stressor hits. This can lead to lower immunity and negative emotional consequences, such as developing anxiety, angry outbursts, and burnout.

Relaxation techniques are a great way to trigger this relaxation response and help you manage your stress. These strategies help your body experience relaxation automatically whenever and wherever you are and they help reduce the time spent in stress mode and any damaging effects it may have had.

Tips for starting your relaxation practice

1. Before starting your relaxation practice, it is recommended that you first talk to a doctor, especially if you have any severe or chronic symptoms. Your symptoms could be a sign that you have an underlying condition you are unaware of. So it is best to get a full diagnosis of your health before commencing. For instance, if your anxiety persists, seeking medical help will help determine whether it is acute/chronic or if it is a symptom of another condition, such as chronic stress or anxiety disorder. Knowing this, you can use your relaxation technique to target the underlying condition, rather than just fix the symptoms.
2. Using these techniques requires practice and patience. With methods like meditation or mindfulness, it is hard to get it right

the first time. Also, to truly benefit from these relaxation methods, your practice has to be consistent.

3. Whenever possible, find a cool, quiet place to practice your relaxation techniques. It should also be free of anything that might distract you or divert your attention. There are exceptions, such as when dealing with acute stress. For instance, you may not need to find a quiet room to do some deep breathing exercises while in a stressful situation.

4. Try and practice your relaxation technique at the same time and place every day. This repetition will help get your mind used to it and make it a habit.

5. Find a comfortable position. You can sit with your legs crossed or stretched out, stand, or lie down. Whatever position you choose, make sure you are comfortable because a relaxation session can last anywhere from five minutes to over an hour or even more. Discomfort can easily distract you and affect your relaxation, so make sure you prevent this. Also, wear comfortable clothes, take off your shoes, jewelry, and anything else that you might feel may cause you discomfort. To trigger your relaxation response, you have to get into a relaxed state, and comfort is key.

6. You can choose to close your eyes or focus on a single spot to keep your eyes from wandering in the room.

7. Empty your mind and focus on the focal point of whatever relaxation method you are using. If you are doing breathing exercises, you may focus on your breath, or if you are using progressive muscle relaxation, you will focus on your breath and the sensations in your body, looking for tense areas and working on releasing that tension.

8. Remember, relaxation doesn't have to mean being or sitting still -- it includes anything that helps you relax, even exercise.

9. Keep a practice journal to record your thoughts, feelings, and observations about your practice. It can provide invaluable insight into helping you create the ideal relaxation practice.

10. Be consistent even though you might not practice every day, try and practice often.

Let's take a look at some of these relaxation techniques.

Relaxation techniques

Relaxation methods or techniques are practices whose goal is to relax the body by inducing the relaxation response. Some of these methods include guided imagery or visualization techniques, deep-breathing exercises, biofeedback, and many more. Some of their effects include slower breathing, lower pulse, and blood pressure and an improved sense of well-being.

A lot of research has been done on the different types of relaxation methods and it was found that they can be very helpful in managing several health conditions, including stress. They have also been verified as safe to use for all healthy people, although you should always consult a health care professional before using these methods. They can provide more insight on how you should go about them and also give you other tips and tricks you can use to improve your relaxation practice.

i. Breathing exercises

Scott at *verywellmind.com* writes that deep breathing is a highly effective stress relieving and relaxation method. Breathing exercises are highly recommended because they can work anywhere and at any time, even in the middle of stressful situations. Becoming aware of your breath can help you be more in tune with your body and its stress response and notice when you need to relax your breathing. They are extremely simple, convenient, and effective. In chapter two, we looked at how to do breathing exercises in general, but there are several different types of breathing exercises you can try. Let's take a look at a few of them:

- **Pursed lip breathing** – This method makes you slow your breathing down by making a deliberate effort every time you breathe. To do it, relax your shoulders and keep your mouth closed as you slowly inhale through your nose for two seconds. Pucker your lips like you are trying to whistle then exhale slowly through your mouth for four seconds. Repeat this method four to five times a day.

- **Mindful diaphragmic breathing** – This method helps you use your diaphragm properly and, hence, breathe more deeply. When starting, you may tire easily, but it will get easier as you advance. Lie flat on your back and slightly bend your knees. You can place a pillow under your knees if you need some support. Place your right hand on your upper chest and the other under your ribcage. This will allow you to feel how your diaphragm moves when you breathe. Inhale slowly and feel how your stomach presses into your hand. While keeping your other hand as still as possible, exhale slowly through pursed lips as you clench your stomach muscles to expel as much air as you can.

You can place a book or have someone place their hand on your abdomen to make this exercise harder. Once you learn how to do it while lying down, you can try belly breathing while sitting on a chair and even advance to doing it while performing other duties.

- **Visualization breathing** – This method uses imagery or focus phrases or words to guide your breathing. For instance, get into a comfortable position just like in diaphragmic breathing and, as you inhale, imagine your abdomen is a balloon filling with air. As you exhale, visualize the air escaping from the balloon slowly. You don't even have to force it out -- it escapes on its own. Alternatively, as you inhale, you can also imagine all of the stress and tension you are feeling moving from your body into your chest. As you exhale, see the stress leave your body through your breath and dissipate the tension. You can also use phrases such as, "I am inhaling calm," or "I am letting go of my stress", as you breathe in and out. You can start practicing with a 10-minute session every day and gradually increase the duration of your sessions.

Other breathing techniques include the counted breathing method, also known as the 4-7-8 method, alternate nostril breathing, lion's breath, equal breathing, coherent breathing, and more. Most of these breathing exercises can be done immediately, so enjoy yourself as you experiment with these different techniques.

Tips on deep breathing

- Let your abdomen expand and contract, instead of moving your shoulders. Breathing this way is deeper and similar to how babies breathe, thus more natural. It allows for increased lung capacity, unlike the shallow breathing we normally do.
- Don't quicken or slow your breathing down too much -- breathe as you normally would, just more deeply.
- Start by doing it for about 5 to 10 minutes a day and increase it as you get more used to the technique. You can start with 2 minutes if five feel like too long.
- If your thoughts drift, don't get alarmed or worried that you are doing it wrong. Rather, notice that you have drifted and refocus on your breath.

ii. Meditation

When it comes to relieving stress, meditation is a powerful skill to have because it works on calming the mind and body while helping you build resilience. Ideal for both acute and chronic stress management, meditation is a helpful skill to have. This ancient practice can take many forms, such as spiritual meditation, mindfulness meditation, focused meditation, movement meditation, mantra meditation, and transcendental meditation.

1. Mindfulness meditation

Mindfulness meditation is a type of meditation that aims at making you more aware of the present moment. By switching your focus to what is happening right now, you can engage fully in what you are doing. You are attentive to your thoughts as they pass through your mind, but you don't engage them or become judgmental of them. You are just an observer taking note of any patterns that might come up. Mindfulness combines concentration with awareness and, as you practice, you might find that focusing on an object or your breath helps you focus on your thoughts, sensations, or emotions. Mindfulness meditation uses meditation techniques to cultivate mindfulness and relieve stress, anxiety, and other conditions and it also helps build resilience, as noted in the *HelpGuide.org* article, "Relaxation Techniques for Stress Relief." You can combine it with other activities, such as walking or exercising.

How to practice mindfulness meditation

When you are beginning your meditation session, find a quiet place, free of disturbances, and make sure you are sitting comfortably with your back straight. Close your eyes and pick a focal point -- this can be your breath or a mantra that you can repeat as you meditate. Don't get worried about any distracting thoughts that might be going through your mind or about how you are doing. Doing this will beat the purpose of this relaxation technique. Instead of fighting them, let them be and return your attention to your focal point.

2. Body scan meditation

This meditation technique directs your attention to various parts of your body. Much like progressive muscle relaxation, you start at your feet and work your way to the top of your body. However, rather than tensing and relaxing your various muscles, you focus on how each part of your body feels, without defining the feeling as good or bad.

How to practice body scan meditation

a. Lie on your back with your legs outstretched and keep your hands at your sides. You can choose to close your eyes or leave them open and find a focal point to concentrate on. Using your preferred breathing technique, focus on your breathing for about three minutes or until you feel yourself starting to relax.

b. Now, turn your attention to the toes on your right foot. Take notice of any sensations you feel as you also pay attention to your breathing. Imagine that each deep breath flows to your toes and remain focused on them for about 5 to 10 seconds.

c. Direct your attention to another part of your foot, such as the sole, and repeat the step above. After about two minutes, move on to your ankle, calf, knee, thigh, hip, and do the same for your left leg. Afterward, you can move to other parts of your body and take note of any pain or discomfort.

d. Once you are done with the whole body, lie still and relax for a bit in silence, while taking note of how your body feels now. After about five minutes, open your eyes, and stretch your body if necessary.

Getting the hang of any meditation technique takes time and a lot of trial and error and not all styles are right for everyone since they require different abilities and mindsets. So maintaining realistic expectations as you start your meditation practice can really help you find the right technique for you.

iii. Visualization

This method is also referred to as guided imagery. It is a form of meditation that involves picturing a scene in your mind where you are safe, free, and at peace -- a place where you can let go of all your tension, stress, fear, and anxiety. As stated before, you can practice visualization either by yourself, use an app, or an audio or visual recording to guide you through the imagery. You can also add soothing music or sounds to help you make the image more realistic.

Practicing visualization, as explained in the article "Visualization and Guided Imagery Techniques for Stress Reduction", requires that you close your eyes and imagine yourself in your restful place. Try to imagine it as vividly as you can. Think of everything you see, hear, taste, smell, or even feel. Incorporating as many of your senses as possible into your visualization helps make it more effective. For instance, if you are thinking about a tropical beach, see the sun rising over the water, hear the birds sing, smell and taste the salty ocean air, and feel the warm waves splash on your feet.

Let this sensation overwhelm you and wash away your worries as you explore your tropical island. When you feel totally relaxed, open your eyes and come back to the present moment. Don't worry if you zone out or forget where you are during your session -- this is absolutely normal. You might also feel some heaviness in your limbs, twitching in your muscles, or even find yourself yawning. Again it is normal to have these responses when you are deeply relaxed.

Other relaxation methods you can try include exercise or rhythmic movements, such as dancing, walking, swimming, or running. You can also give yourself a massage to ease tensions in your body. It is important to make these relaxation methods part of your regular life. As you practice them more regularly, your body becomes more skilled at handling and even reversing its stress response when necessary, so you do not remain stressed for long periods.

CHAPTER NINE:

Mindfulness Techniques - Relieving Stress In The Moment

By now, you have probably noticed that I mention mindfulness a lot throughout this book. Mindfulness is defined as the capacity to be present and fully cognizant of our actions and where we are and not reacting or getting overwhelmed by what's going on in our environment. While it is an ability we all naturally possess, our capacity to readily utilize it comes from practicing it every day. Mindfulness aims to awaken the inner workings of our physical, mental, and emotional processes. Therefore, it can be used to help relieve stress, which can disrupt these processes. These methods are referred to as mindfulness techniques. Let's take a deeper look at them.

What is Mindfulness-Based Stress Reduction (MBSR)?

MBSR can be described as a program that aims to help participants gain mindfulness and thus change how they handle stress and reduce its effects. This program was created by Jon Kabat-Zinn in 1979 to help in the treatment of people suffering from stress, depression, anxiety, and other mental conditions. He theorized that getting patients to work on the mindfulness exercises in a group format would help develop their ability to view their pain more objectively and also learn how to relate to it differently, thus suffer from it less.

This quote, from psychiatrist Viktor Frankl, can help explain how it works: "There is a space between stimulus and response. That space contains our power to choose how we respond and our growth and freedom lies in our response." Simply put, there is a moment where we can choose how to react to stressors or pain before we actually react to them. However, many of us are unaware of this space because we get caught up in our habitual patterns and reactions to life.

If someone cuts you off on the highway, you might think, "What is wrong with that person", but your heart is already beating faster and your grip on the wheel has gotten tighter. You get angry and this anger feeds your thoughts and now you think that this person deserves to be taught a lesson. So you speed up next to him and get into a staredown and even exchange heated words, letting him know that you know what he did.

This is an example of a stressful situation fueled by a continuous, unconscious interaction between our habits, emotions, and thoughts. You might argue that you didn't have much of an option in the situation because you might have been unaware of your stress reaction, however, the space we mentioned earlier was there between the moment you were cut off and how you reacted. In his article "Mindfulness-Based Stress Reduction: What It Is, How It Helps", Baum notes that MBSR helps us become more aware of our habitual reactions and assists us in relating to ourselves in a different way to disrupt this cycle and give us more choices. After this reflection, you may realize that reacting to the guy who cut off on the highway only worsened your stress and may not have affected him as it did you, or maybe you made him angrier, which could escalate the situation.

In the future, if something happens while you are driving and you notice your grip tighten, your pulse quicken, or you start breathing faster, try to take the moment to realize that your body is alerting you that a stress reaction is happening. Now, you are in the space between stimulus and response, where you can choose to take a few breaths and pacify yourself and to relax your shoulders and hands. You could even consider the bad state the other driver must be in for him to drive that way. You could wish him well because if he were in a good state, he wouldn't be driving like that. By adopting the techniques taught in MBSR, you begin to see that you can change the long-held fears that may have been holding you back.

MBSR is a customizable and adaptable approach to relieving stress and it is comprised of three main components, namely mindfulness meditation, body scanning, and yoga. Rather than follow the steps stipulated for the practice, you practice it in the manner that best suits you. This means that MBSR is different for everyone, even though it is based on the same principles.

The Center for Mindfulness gives the following necessities for practicing MBSR:

- Turning the experience into a challenge instead of a chore. This changes the observation of your life from something else you have to do to be healthy to something you look forward to -- an adventure.
- The emphasis of consistency in your practice and the importance of individual effort and motivation. What this means is practicing even on a day you don't feel like it.
- A lifestyle change is needed once you start the program because it requires a significant time commitment. The program is eight weeks long and participants need to practice about six days a week for 45 minutes daily and also attend weekly meetings that could last over two hours. You may also have to take a day-long retreat and have a seven-hour mindfulness session.

To practice MBSR, Kabat-Zinn gives the following foundational attitudes that are essential to the practice:

- A non-judgmental attitude
- Patience
- Trust
- A beginner's mind
- Acceptance
- Learning to let go and not striving to be perfect

MBSR can be used alone or combined with other methods to relieve stress and other conditions that might induce stress effectively. However, there are some things you should keep in mind before starting your mindfulness practice:

1. When you begin, you will find that it is different than what you were expecting. So it is important to maintain realistic expectations. You might end up pleasantly surprised, but keep an open mind and understand that while mindfulness is a wonderful technique, it is not a cure-all.
2. Mindfulness is not about fixing you, but rather it is about noticing your thoughts, actions, habits, and feelings.
3. It is also not about stopping your thoughts, but rather about helping you become aware of them and changing them to better, healthier thoughts, emotions, actions, and habits.
4. Some people are wary of trying mindfulness out because they think practicing it means that they have converted to another religion. This is not true. Even though MBSR is based on Buddhist principles, it is not part of any religion.
5. It is not a way to escape your reality, but rather to change it.
6. It does more than just reduce your stress -- it can help your body thrive and boost your creativity.
7. Mindfulness can also boost your neural connections, help you build new neural circuits, boost your concentration, awareness, and flexibility.

Mindfulness techniques and exercises

As expected, mindfulness makes up a big part of most MBSR techniques and it is easy to think of it as a state of mind. These exercises are aimed at helping you become more mindful by emphasizing different areas. If you are interested in doing mindfulness meditation but don't know where to start, why not try some of these mindfulness exercises. Some of them can even be done in less than five minutes.

Techniques

- Focused mindfulness – An important aspect of mindfulness is the ability to calm and focus your mind. Focused mindfulness, therefore, emphasizes on focusing on what's happening internally and observing your mind. It can be likened to keeping your eyes on the road by focusing on a particular occurrence. You can choose to focus on your breath, bodily sensations, or an object to keep you grounded in the present moment.
- Cognizance or awareness mindfulness – Unlike focused mindfulness, this technique emphasizes looking outwards rather than inwards. It entails looking at your mind from an outside perspective. When trying the awareness approach, you view your mental activity as if it belonged to someone else. Put differently, it can be described as observing your thoughts and emotions from outside your usual self-centered point of view. You view your mind as a consciousness stream without attaching any judgment to it.

You can also switch between these two techniques. To do this, take notice of your consciousness, rationally, and select something to focus on or become aware of.

Exercises

This section outlines some of the exercises you can use to develop your mindfulness.

1. Breathing exercises – These exercises facilitate mindfulness by helping you focus on your breath. In the previous chapter, we explored deep breathing in-depth and stated a few breathing techniques you can use to help develop your mindfulness.

2. Body-scan meditation – This exercise involves becoming aware of the sensations in your body. Body-scan meditation allows you to transfer your awareness throughout your body by focusing on a single body part at a time. When you find an especially tense or sore area, use your breath and focus on this area until you

relax. You can even combine it with a healing visualization, such as a ball of warm light melting the soreness away. We also looked at how to practice body-scan meditation in chapter eight, so you can refer to this technique here, as well.

3. Object meditation – This involves focusing your attention on an object. You can use something special to you if it helps you focus more. Hold it in your hand and let it be the center of your attention. Direct all your senses to it and take note of the sensations you observe. These can include its color, taste, smell, shape, texture, size, or even the sound it makes when you manipulate it, either by squeezing, hitting, dropping it, and so on.

4. Walking meditation – This involves developing mindfulness as you take a leisurely meditative walk. As you take your leisurely walk, keep a calm pace and take note of how you are walking. Is your back straight? Do you swing your hands? Or do you swing your hips a bit? Also, focus on the sensations you feel as you walk. Are your shoulders feeling tight or loose? How are your feet touching the ground? At the end of the path, turn and continue walking while maintaining your awareness of these sensations.

5. Mindful eating – This exercise calls for you to pay attention to what you are eating. Take note of what you are holding, how it feels in your hand, how heavy it feels, the color, smell, etc. Then move on to eating it, but do this slowly as you savor how it tastes, the way its texture feels on your tongue, and its smell. This exercise can help you discover new sensations using familiar foods.

A great example of mindful eating is the raisin exercise. It is a great introductory exercise for those looking to try mindfulness. You can use any food you want, as long as it has an unusual smell, taste, or feel to it. Take a raisin and imagine that you have never seen one before. Pay attention to how it looks, feels, smells, how the skin moves when you touch it. Then, eat it.

While it's in your mouth, savor how it tastes, the way the skin feels on your tongue and how the taste changes when you chew on it. Let it linger and then swallow it.

By focusing on the raisin or whatever food you are mindfully eating, you are less likely to spend time or waste energy and attention on worrying about what was stressing you. This exercise helps you take notice of what is in front of you and focuses your attention on it. Even if your mind wanders, you can guide it back to the exercise.

6. Take 10 seconds every hour to yawn and stretch. Yawn, even if it's fake -- it will trigger a real one. Breathe in deeply and exhale, saying, "ahh". Notice how your yawn disrupts your thoughts and centers your focus on the present. Next, stretch slowly for another 1- seconds. Take non-judgmental notice of the tense areas and say to them "ease". Do this for about 20 to 30 seconds then resume what you were doing.

7. Stretching mindfully – You can practice applying mindfulness to any stretching exercises you want, but if you are looking for a guided version, then try yoga. Many videos can be used for guided yoga practice and, once you get used to them and know the poses, you can move to audio recordings or practice without any guidance.

8. STOP – This acronym means Stop, Take a Breath, Observe, and Proceed. Jon Kabat Zinn, the pioneer of this meditation technique suggests you:

First, stand up and breathe. This allows you to feel your connection to the ground.

Secondly, tune into your body. Look at yourself and scan your body, taking notice of all your sensations, thoughts, and emotions. Use your breath to release negative thoughts, emotions, and sensations, such as tension, and occupy your mind with pleasant ones as you breathe in.

Thirdly, observe. Use your eyes to look at your surroundings and take it in. Take notice of something beautiful and be grateful for it.

Lastly, think of the possibility. Explore your possibilities by asking what's new, what steps can be taken as you move forward, or what is possible.

If you find yourself reacting to any of these steps, pause and take a few deep breaths. You can also repeat the following phrases, "calm down", or "clear head" and take in more deep breaths as you exhale saying "melt", "relax", and other calming words.

9. Try loving-kindness meditation – This exercise involves repeating phrases that highlight your good qualities in yourself and others. In other words, it means being kind to yourself and others. You can start by delighting in your goodness. Think of the deeds you have done out of the goodness of your heart, rejoicing in their memory, and celebrating your potential for good. Now silently repeat phrases that idealize what you'd wish for most earnestly.

    For instance, repeat the following phrases: "May I be physically, mentally, and emotionally whole", "May I forgive", "May I live with ease", and so on. Repeat these words in a pattern that pleases you, paying attention to one phrase at a time. If your thoughts wander, that is fine, just refocus. Now visualize yourself in the midst of those who have been kind to you or whose kindness has inspired you. See yourself as the recipient of their love and kindness as you keep repeating the phrases. As the session ends, let go of the visualization but keep repeating the words for a bit longer. In doing so, you are transforming the hurtful relationship you had with yourself and now you can move towards a kinder future.

There are very few things that can stop you from practicing MBSR because, if you have a mind, you can practice mindfulness and if your body is capable of moving, you can do yoga. Through mindfulness meditation, we can address current stressors and also help us develop our resilience to future stressors. It can help us get healthier while gaining a deeper, lasting sense of peace.

- Not enough control over job-related decisions; no control over how you do your work
- Conflicting demands or unclear performance expectations; unclear on how to handle certain tasks; let down by a colleague because they did not perform how you wanted

Some of the warning signs of work-related stress include:

- Increased anxiety, irritability, or even depression
- Indifference and losing interest in your work
- Inability to sleep; you keep tossing and turning
- Fatigue, even after getting up in the morning
- Trouble concentrating on anything
- Muscle tension or headaches
- Problems with your stomach
- Withdrawing socially
- Loss of sex drive
- Abuse of alcohol and drugs to help you quiet the thoughts and cope

Dean was working in what he thought was his ideal job. He had worked hard to get there, staying long hours at the office, working while at home and even during the weekends, and spent a lot of time away from his family and friends. All his hard work didn't go unnoticed and soon he got an offer from another company. They offered him a senior post, managing a small group. Dean was thrilled. Shortly after starting his new job, he noticed that the pressure to perform was always there. He had demands from upper management and also pressures from managing a team and their various needs. His home life was also chaotic since he and his wife had just had a baby girl and she was not sleeping well, which meant that they weren't sleeping well either. This was causing a lot of tension at home.

His team was put in charge of a very important ad campaign and a lot was riding on it and making a good presentation to their clients. Dean was already on edge since he wasn't sleeping that well, he couldn't eat, and his mind was racing. He felt like he didn't have time to do anything anymore and his concentration was dwindling. He couldn't think through problems that were brought to his attention and he started getting sick a lot, too. Now he had to oversee this big project and that only added to the pressure he felt.

On the day of the presentation, Jamie, one of Dean's interns, spilled coffee on his desk, soaking a few of his presentation notes, just as he was leaving for the meeting. Dean snapped. He started shouting at Jamie, causing a scene as everyone wondered why sweet Dean was tearing off poor Jamie's head. But then something happened. During his outburst, he suddenly clutched his chest and collapsed. He was rushed to the emergency room, where doctors determined that he had suffered a heart attack.

When he regained consciousness, the doctor told him what happened and he told Dean that what was really affecting him was the stress and pressure he was under. It's what caused the heart attack. This served as a wakeup call to Dean that he needed to change. So, when he got discharged, he started seeing a counselor who helped him identify his stressors and taught him different ways he could deal with stress, whether at home or work. He learned how to prioritize better and only take on what he could handle. He went back to exercising, something he loved, and watched what he ate. These few changes made a big difference over time and helped him lead a better life and attain a new level of job satisfaction.

When you feel that your job is demanding too much from you and you have no control over it, you are at risk of getting diseases, such as heart disease or high blood pressure. The severity of your job stress depends on its demands, your sense of control, and the decision-making state of mind you are in when handling the demands. Can you identify some of Dean's stressors? Let's look at the different ways you can manage your stress and see if you could identify a few that could have helped Dean out.

Ways you can manage stress at your workplace

Job-related stress doesn't just disappear once you get home. It can persist and take a toll on your health and well-being. Uncontrolled stress can cause you to have headaches, an upset stomach, sleeplessness, a shorter temper, and difficulty concentrating. If it persists, you can get anxiety, depression, insomnia, stomach problems, cardiovascular issues, and because you have lowered immunity, opportunistic infections. How you choose to deal with your stress can compound your condition, such as overeating, eating a lot of junk food, or abusing alcohol and drugs.

While stress at work is expected, excessive stress can affect your productivity and performance. Whatever your work demands of you, according to the American Psychological Association, there are techniques, skills, and steps you can take to protect yourself from its harmful effects, boost your well-being, and give you more job satisfaction in and out of where you work. Let's look at some of them.

1.   Track your stressors

Take note of things that might be inducing stress at your workplace. By identifying your stressors, you can easily find ways to relieve or avoid them. You can keep a journal for about a week and identify any situations that created stress and also note how you responded to them. Record your thoughts, feelings, and any information about the situation, also noting the people and circumstances involved. Think about how you reacted -- did you raise your voice? Did you think of eating? Or did you go out for a walk? Taking note of these reactions, they can help identify underlying patterns among your stressors and how you habitually react to them.

2.   Have healthy responses

Sit back and think about how you respond to stressors. If you find yourself in a stressful situation at work, do you have an angry outburst, stuff your feelings away, walk away, or try to eat or drink your feelings away? Or do you confront whomever it is that might be causing you problems? Rather than using these negative ways to fight stress, why not try responding more healthily? There are many things you can do to relieve stress, such as exercise, yoga, meditation, eating a healthy diet, or deep breathing.

You can also make time for your hobbies and other favorite activities, such as reading a book, going to a concert, playing games, and so forth. Setting aside this time to spend on something you like doing something or with people you love can greatly reduce your stress levels. By developing healthy ways to respond to stress, you reduce its adverse effects on your body and the strain it puts on you and others.

3. Create boundaries

In today's world, it is easy to feel pressure because we are connected 24/7. So, it is important to develop some work-life balance by establishing some boundaries for yourself. This could mean not taking your work home, checking your emails, or your phone during family time or answering work calls while at home. Everybody has different preferences when it comes to how much they value their work or home life. But creating very clear boundaries between these two worlds reduces the chances for conflict and the stress that ensues.

4. Prioritize and organize

You don't have to do everything by yourself. Learn to prioritize, organize, and delegate tasks to lighten your workload. Taken on high-priority tasks first and break them down to tackle them more easily. Delegate duties and be more accommodating. Create a balanced schedule and take enough time to spend with your family, on social activities, other responsibilities, and downtime to prevent burnout. Learn to leave earlier, plan regular breaks, and establish healthy boundaries. Also, do not over commit yourself to a task. It is okay to say you may not be able and not feel like you will be letting people down. Understand what you should be doing and what you must be doing and drop unnecessary tasks.

5. Break bad habits

If you think about it, it is our negative thoughts and behaviors that often make job stress worse for us. If you can change them, you can decrease your stress and improve your working conditions. Resist the urge for perfectionism in everything you do because you are only setting yourself up for frustration. Rather, have realistic goals and expectations, do your best, and be okay with quality work. You can't control everything, so don't try to. Learn how to be okay with that. If you lack the motivation or the energy needed to work, try changing how you think about your job. Be more positive, stay away from negative coworkers, and always appreciate the small achievements you make, even if no one else does.

6. Take time to recharge

Take time off and relax. This can help avoid burnout and also keep you motivated and energized. Your body needs time to recover, so set aside time when you don't engage in work-related activities or even think about work. Make use of your vacation days and go somewhere to relax. This disconnection is critical in helping you unwind.

7. Sleep well

You must get a good night's sleep. Skimping on sleep interferes with your productivity, creativity, and your ability to solve problems and focus. When you are rested, you are better equipped to handle your job responsibilities and cope with stress. Find ways to improve the quality of your sleep. It is not about the number of hours you sleep, but the quality of the sleep. Try to sleep and wake up at the same time every day, even during the weekend, avoid caffeine a few hours before you sleep, and change your bedroom to make it more conducive to sleep.

Try and get about eight hours of sleep. This is the amount recommended for most adults. Turn off your TV screen, tablet, phones, computers, and other electronic devices that can suppress your body's production of melatonin and affect your circadian (sleep/wake) rhythm. Engage in soothing, calming activities before bed, such as reading, listening to music, or meditating, rather than trying to catch up on work before you sleep.

8. Reach out to someone

Consider getting some support by accepting help from friends, family members, and even coworkers you trust to build resilience and your ability to manage work-related stress. However, if you continue feeling overwhelmed, consider talking to a mental health care professional, such as a psychologist, who can help you get to the root of the problem, alter your self-destructive behavior, and get your stress under control.

9. Be proactive about your job

Regaining some control over your job or your career can help you manage your stress. Consider talking to your supervisor about the stressors in your workplace. Since many companies are aware of the detrimental effects stress can have on their workforce, they are proactive in fighting it.

Ask for a clear description of what your job entails, your responsibilities, and duties. This way, you will not be assigned something that is out of the parameters of your job. You can also request a transfer to escape a toxic environment. If you feel that your current job does not offer you any way to advance in your career, why not ask for new duties? Look for job satisfaction and find meaning in your work. This could mean a different list of duties, working in a different department, and so on.

10. Learn how to relax

Learn more about the different techniques you can use to relieve and manage stress, such as meditation, breathing exercises, and mindfulness. Take a look at the previous chapters to see the many different techniques that you can use to deal with your stress and how to practice them.

If Dean had applied some of these techniques, such as keeping up with exercise, finding ways to solve his sleeping problem, talking to his supervisor about getting some help on the ad project, eating better, and taking better care of himself, maybe he would have been able to handle that coffee situation and his overall stress a lot better.

Simple tips that can help reduce your work-related stress:

- Start the day off right, preferably with some meditation to get you in the right mindset
- Have a clear list of requirements for your job and the tasks you are delegating to others
- Avoid conflict, but where you can't deal with it, don't let it fester
- Keep yourself organized, clear any mess on your desk, and plan out what you have to do
- Don't try and do too many things at once
- Take a nature walk during your lunch and mindfully engage in walking meditation
- Don't be a perfectionist or a procrastinator
- Listen to music to soothe you

FINAL WORDS

In our technologically advanced world, we are faced with threats and demands that can trigger our stress response and the cascade of unhealthy biological reactions that ensue, resulting in stress. As I stated before, this can lead to a slew of stress-related diseases, some of which include cardiovascular conditions, anxiety disorders, depression, obesity, and a host of other conditions triggered by low immunity and disrupted digestion processes. This book teaches you the different ways you can mitigate your stress, its effects, and learn how to control it.

You might be hard-pressed to find a collection of stress reduction and management techniques like those collected in this book. They are a combination of mind and body calming techniques aimed at teaching you how you can respond to stress differently. They are backed by science and are also practical, written in an engaging, easy to read format that allows you to pinpoint exactly what you are looking for. If you need quick ways to relieve stress, just jump to chapter two or try some of the relaxation techniques in chapter eight. This book also teaches psychological practices, such as meditation and mindfulness, that can help combat unhealthy reactions to stress while building your resilience.

I've covered a lot throughout this book, but let's recap some of the major points:

Chapter one was all about the basics of stress. What is stress? How do our bodies react to it? What is the stress response? What takes place during a stress response? And what are some of the causes of stress? We defined stress as to how we react to the demands of changes in our environment and it can be good or bad. We looked at the different types of stress, such as acute stress and chronic stress. Acute stress is also known as short-term stress and it is what we feel when we are in a stressful situation, but it quickly goes away. Chronic stress, on the other hand, doesn't. You may not even be aware that is suffering from chronic stress -- you might think that the situation you are in is normal. However, after studying this book, it should be clear that the constant pressure you feel is not good for you and something should be done about it.

Chapter two is an overview of some of the few stress management techniques you can use. It includes a breakdown of quick stress relievers and other long-term techniques to help build your resilience to stress. The third chapter showed you how to identify stressors. These are the factors contributing to your stress. By going through a simple list of the known stressors that I listed or by journaling, you can pinpoint what is inducing your stress. Chapter four looked at the four pillars of stress management. By understanding what each of these pillars entails, you are able to learn when it is best to avoid a stressor, alter it, adapt to it, or accept it.

In subsequent chapters, we looked at how to worry less and enjoy your life more, find out what might be worrying you, and how to deal with it. We also looked at what emotional resilience and mental toughness are and how you can build them to help you combat stress. By developing emotional resilience and mental toughness, you are better equipped to tackle anything that comes your way and you are not easily affected by it. We also took a look at different relaxation techniques and how you can also use them to boost your emotional resilience and mental toughness. We explored how to apply mindfulness in the techniques we use to relieve stress and, finally, we looked at work-related stress and how you can manage it.

All of the techniques mentioned in this book are guaranteed to help you better manage your stress. I showed you how you could use techniques such as mindfulness, meditation, and relaxation methods to help build your resilience and stay calm under pressure. This way, you can look at the situation objectively rather than subjectively and, in doing so, gain a different perspective on it. You can then come up with new ways on how to deal with your situation.

So rather than sitting at your desk, worried about how much work you have to get done, why not organize your tasks in order of importance and focus on those first. If you can delegate the work, that's even better. However, you have to remember that we all have different standards, so don't expect that everyone will meet yours. What is perfect to me may still need some work, according to you. But ask yourself, were the conditions of the task you assigned met? If the answer is yes and the work is good enough, accept it. Letting go of perfectionism will take away a lot of the unnecessary stress you put on yourself and others.

The most valuable take away from this book is that you don't have to suffer through your stress. By applying the techniques in this book, you can regain control over your work and home life and improve their quality. Take action against stress now and start living your life to the fullest.

RESOURCES

The American Institute of Stress. (n.d.). Retrieved from https://www.stress.org/what-is-stress

Mayo Clinic Staff. (2017, March 31). Stress management. Retrieved from https://www.mayoclinic.org/healthy-lifestyle/stress-management/basics/stress-basics/hlv-20049495

Alarm Stage of Stress: Definition & Explanation. (2015, June 16). Retrieved from https://study.com/academy/lesson/alarm-stage-of-stress-definition-lesson-quiz.html.

Higuera, V. (n.d.). What Is General Adaptation Syndrome? Retrieved May 1, 2017, from https://www.healthline.com/health/general-adaptation-syndrome#definition

Felman, A. (2017, November 28). Why stress happens and how to manage it. Retrieved from https://www.medicalnewstoday.com/articles/145855.php#what_is_stress

DeMorrow S. (2018, March 26). Role of the Hypothalamic-Pituitary-Adrenal Axis in Health and Disease. International journal of molecular sciences, 19(4), 986. doi:10.3390/ijms19040986

Mayo Clinic Staff. (2019, March 28). Stress management. Retrieved from https://www.mayoclinic.org/healthy-lifestyle/stress-management/in-depth/stress-management/art-20044151

Scott, E. (2019, September 11). 5 Ways to Calm Down Quickly When You're Feeling Overwhelmed. Retrieved from https://www.verywellmind.com/ways-to-calm-down-quickly-when-overwhelmed-3145197

Scott, E. (2019, October 8). An Overview of Stress Management. Retrieved from https://www.verywellmind.com/stress-management-4157211

Moore, C. (2019, June 28). What Is Mindfulness? Definition + Benefits (Incl. Psychology). Retrieved from https://positivepsychology.com/what-is-mindfulness/

YOUR FREE GIFT

Thank you again for purchasing this book. As an additional thank you, you will receive an e-book, as a gift, and completely free.

This guide gives you 14 Days of Mindfulness and sets you on a two-week course to staying present and relaxed. Practice each of the daily prompts to learn more about mindfulness, and add it to your daily routine and meditations.

You can get the bonus booklet as follows:

To access the secret download page, open a browser window on your computer or smartphone and enter: **bonus.derickhowell.com**

You will be automatically directed to the download page.

Please note that this bonus booklet may be only available for download for a limited time.

Printed in Great Britain
by Amazon

37423209R00068